It's another Quality Book from CGP

This book has been carefully written for Key Stage Two children preparing for the reading part of the Year 6 SATs. It's full of tricky questions covering all seven of the reading Assessment Focuses:

AF1 Understand the **meaning** of a text ⟵

AF1 isn't specifically tested in the SAT, but it underpins all the other Assessment Focuses.

AF2 Select and **retrieve** information

AF3 **Infer** information and ideas

AF4 Understand **structural** and **layout** features

AF5 Understand **language** features

AF6 Interpret the **writer's purpose**

AF7 Relate texts to their **context**

In this book we've separated the questions out so children can learn how to spot questions on each Assessment Focus and give exactly the right kind of answer.

Children can use the Reading Raptor tick boxes for self-assessment, which helps you work out how they're getting on with each Assessment Focus.

Published by CGP

Editors:
Claire Boulter, Joe Brazier, Camilla Simson,
Megan Tyler and Rachel Ward.

*Many thanks to Judy Hornigold and
Luke von Kotze for proofreading.*

ISBN: 978 1 84146 163 2

Groovy website: www.cgpbooks.co.uk
Jolly bits of clipart from CorelDRAW®
Printed by Elanders Ltd, Newcastle upon Tyne.

Based on the classic CGP style created by Richard Parsons.

Psst... photocopying this Workbook isn't allowed, even if you've got a CLA licence. Luckily, it's dead cheap, easy and quick to order more copies from CGP – just call us on 0870 750 1242. Phew!

AF2 Fact Retrieval Questions

These FACT RETRIEVAL questions just ask you to pick out information from the text.
Have another read of Eureka! and then try and find the answers to these questions.

1. The introduction to the booklet tells us

that inventors are often normal people	that inventors go to a special inventors' school	that only five people invented everything	that there are no such things as inventors

1 mark

Circle your answer.

2. Use the information from the text to match up the inventors to what they invented. The first one has been done for you.

2 marks

Marconi — Invented the telephone

Alexander Graham Bell — Invented the radio

Farnsworth — Invented aeroplanes

The Wright Brothers — Invented television

3. How were 'cats' eyes' invented?

a man was driving in a car and he had his ~~fish~~ heads lights on and they ~~but~~ Shon on a pairof cats eyes and the lights reflected off them.

2 marks

4. What did the crowd do when the Wright brothers managed to make their first plane fly?

The spectators gasped and there was an enomos round of aplos.

1 mark

5. Was Isaac Newton an accidental inventor or a born inventor?

Isaac Newton was a born inventor.

1 mark

Keep turning... ➡

Eureka!

Have you ever looked around you at all the things you have in your house and wondered how they got there? Who invented them? Why were they invented?

Inventors are usually ordinary people like you and me who discover something that needs changing or improving. Sometimes people don't even know they are inventors until they discover a problem they want to solve. If nobody else is willing to sort out their problem then they do it themselves and lo and behold, a new invention appears.

Born Inventors

Sometimes, people are so curious that they can't help themselves. For example, when Sir Isaac Newton discovered that light was made up of all the colours of the rainbow, he spent months investigating his theory and setting up experiments that separated the light into its different colours. He wouldn't stop until his work was done.

Sir Isaac Newton

Cats' eyes — the inspiration

Accidental Inventors

Other inventors come across their ideas purely by accident. The little glass marbles in the middle of roads that reflect the light from car headlights and help drivers to follow the road in the night are called 'cats' eyes'. The inventor got his idea when driving at night and he noticed that his car headlights were reflecting in the eyes of a cat sitting by the side of the road. And so another life-changing invention was born.

Where To Begin?

It takes a while for an idea to develop into a full-blown product, being sold in the shops. Follow the arrows below to track an invention from idea to shop floor.

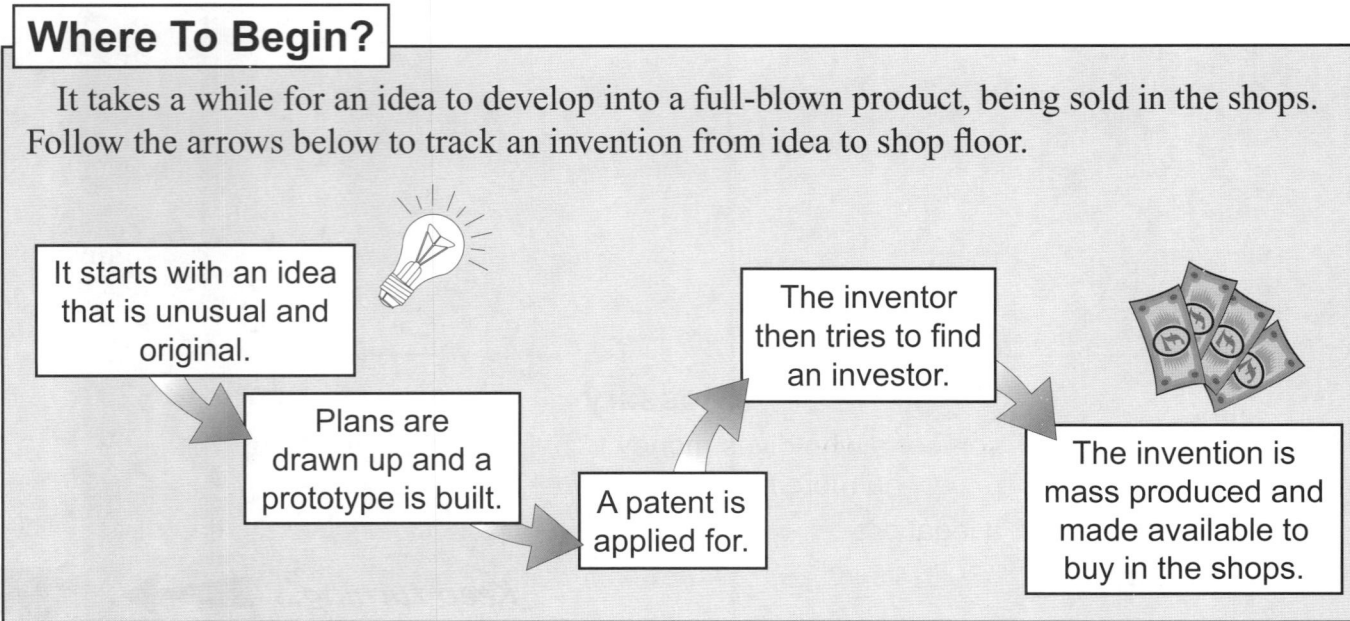

It starts with an idea that is unusual and original.

Plans are drawn up and a prototype is built.

A patent is applied for.

The inventor then tries to find an investor.

The invention is mass produced and made available to buy in the shops.

Believing In What You Have Invented

It's not easy to be a successful inventor, but everything you see around you every day, from televisions to mobile phones, were invented by someone. Every invention also went through the same process of idea to product.

The Television

The hardest part of the invention process is believing in what you are making. When Marconi invented the first radio in 1896 and Farnsworth invented the first television in 1927, people laughed and said they would never be popular!

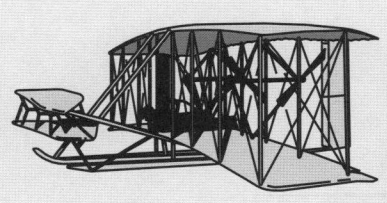

The Aeroplane

The Wright Brothers believed they could invent a machine that would let men fly. Almost everyone said they must be mad, but they knew they could build an aeroplane. In 1902 they held their first successful flight, where spectators gasped and burst into an enormous round of applause. The Wright Brothers believed in their invention and they proved that they were right.

Alexander Graham Bell invented the telephone in 1887. He knew that sound could travel through wires and after many experiments and prototypes, the world's first telephone appeared. This idea was mocked by Bell's friends, but thanks to his hard work, it is now one of the most popular ways of communicating in the world.

The Telephone

What Would We Do Without Them?

Imagine a world without telephones, televisions, radios and aeroplanes. It's difficult because these inventions are so important in our 21st century lives. We would live very different lives if it were not for the dedication of the inventors and the belief they had in their inventions.

We owe a lot to inventors, but it's easy to forget about them when you're sitting in front of your wide-screen television, talking to your friend on the phone.

So the next time you get on a plane, switch on a washing machine, talk on your mobile or switch on your computer, think about the person whose idea it was and the process they went through so you could use it. Maybe they will encourage you to invent something yourself. *Good Luck!*

Glossary

investor	—	someone who gives money to help make the invention, expecting more money back when the invention sells
patent	—	a legal document that stops other people from copying the idea
prototype	—	the first example of a new invention, made to test the design

Eureka! — Non-Fiction

*Non-fiction is any old bit of writing that has facts in and isn't made up.
Non-fiction can be about anything in the universe, from toenail clippings
to Tyrannosaurus Rex. This particular bit of non-fiction's about
<u>inventors</u> and the piles of clever gadgets they've invented.
What on earth would you be doing this evening if televisions had
never been invented? Probably scrubbing turnips down a coal mine.
That's what they used to do for fun in the old days, you know.*

What to do —

1) Open out the folding pages and read
   the non-fiction text *Eureka!*

2) Then read it again. It's the only way
   to be sure you've understood it all.

3) Now have a mental mini-break —
   think about chocolate, letting yourself
   drool just a little. Then wipe your face
   and get on with the questions.

Turn the page ➡

 **AF2** # *Fact Retrieval Questions*

6. Draw lines to match the words to their meanings.

Investor   A document saying an idea can't be copied

Prototype   A model of your original idea

Patent   Someone willing to put money into your invention

2 marks

7. In what year was the telephone invented?

The year the telephone was made was 1887

1 mark

8. What happens to an invention after the inventor finds an investor?

The invention is mass produced and made available to stay in the shops.

1 mark

9. What is an accidental inventor?

Accidental inventors are the inventos come across there Ideas by accident.

1 mark

10. Use information from under the different subheadings to help you fill in this table.
Some of the boxes have already been filled in for you.

Accidental inventors.	Tells us about people who invent things without meaning to.
What Would We Do Without Them?	*It's difficult because these inventions are so important in the 21st century lives.*
Glossary	*A glossary is a listing of terms*
Where To Begin?	Tells us about the invention process from idea to shop.

3 marks

Reading Raptors find facts hidden in the deepest, darkest caves. How did you get on with these pages?

Inference Questions

INFERENCE questions are all about using your imagination and doing a bit of detective work to work out what's going on. Read through Eureka! again and have a go at these questions.

1. At the end, the booklet tells us to

take inventors for granted	be afraid of inventors	look for inventors at school	be thankful to inventors

(be thankful to inventors circled)

1 mark

Circle your answer.

2. The section called **'Believing In What You Have Invented'** is about

having faith in your own work	having faith in the work of others	hoping that you might be successful	just doing it for the fun of it

(having faith in your own work circled)

1 mark

Circle your answer.

3. Draw lines to match the subheadings from the text to the message of each paragraph. One has been done for you.

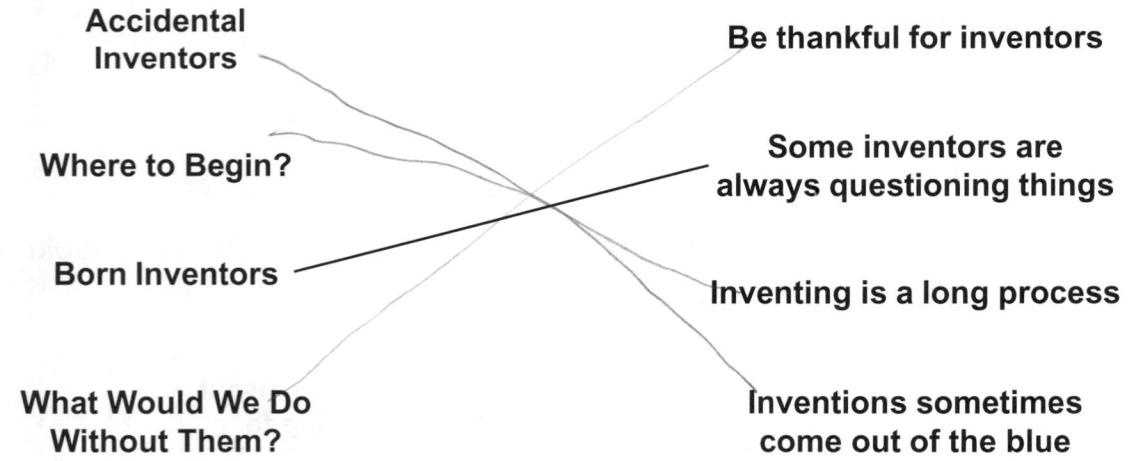

Accidental Inventors

Where to Begin?

Born Inventors

What Would We Do Without Them?

Be thankful for inventors

Some inventors are always questioning things

Inventing is a long process

Inventions sometimes come out of the blue

2 marks

4. What is the difference between 'Born Inventors' and 'Accidental Inventors' according to the article?

Accidental inventors discover thing by accident however

born inventers are naturally curious

2 marks

 **AF3**   *Inference Questions*

5. When the Wright brothers held their first successful flight, the spectators **'gasped'**. What does the word 'gasped' imply about the spectators?

....

....

| 1 |
| mark |

6. Why do you think that inventors and their inventions are mocked and doubted by people they know?

....

....

....

| 2 |
| marks |

7. How do you think inventors feel when their ideas are laughed at?

....

....

| 2 |
| marks |

8. Why do you think that believing in your idea is the hardest part of the process?

....

....

....

| 2 |
| marks |

9. How do you think people might have felt the first time they used a telephone?

....

....

....

| 2 |
| marks |

Reading Raptors can do Inference questions in their sleep. How were your detective skills?

Structure and Layout Questions

Writers often lay their work out to make it clearer, or to **EMPHASISE SOME THINGS** *more than others.* **Have a look through the text for layout features before you try these questions.**

1. Why have the words been put into boxes in the **'Where to Begin?'** section?

   ....

   `1 mark`

2. What is the purpose of the subheadings and how do they help you to understand the text better?

   ....

   `2 marks`

   ....

3. How do the arrows in **'Where to Begin'** help you to understand the text?

   ....

   `1 mark`

4. What is the glossary and how does it help you to understand the text better?

   ....

   `2 marks`

   ....

5. How do the pictures help you to understand the text?

   ....

   `2 marks`

   ....

6. How does the final section, **'What Would We Do Without Them?'**, link back to the opening paragraph?

   ....

   `2 marks`

   ....

Reading Raptors eat Layout questions for breakfast. Sometimes for lunch too. How did you get on?

Writer's Purpose Questions

Writers don't just write random stuff — they think carefully about what they want to say.
Read the text again and think about why the writer wrote each section. Then try these questions.

1. Why do you think the writer started this piece with questions?

1 mark

....

2. 'spectators gasped and burst into an enormous round of applause'

Why do you think the writer chose to tell us this piece of information?

2 marks

....

....

3. 'Maybe they will encourage you to invent something yourself. *Good Luck!*'

Are you encouraged to have a go at inventing after reading the text?

Tick one box and explain your reasons in detail below.

☐ Yes   ☐ No

2 marks

....

....

4. Why do you think the writer included the section 'Believing In What You Have Invented'?

2 marks

....

....

5. Why do you think the writer chose 'cats' eyes' as an example of an invention?

2 marks

....

....

Reading Raptors can read a writer's mind and know exactly what they're thinking. How about you?

INFERENCE means looking at bits of the story and working out what the author really means or what a character is thinking. See if you can work out the answers to these.

1. **'We don't know a millionth of one percent about anything.'**

   What do you think this quote means?

   | 1 mark |

   ....

2. **'When he arrived, both the Morrisons and the creature inside the TV gave a sigh of relief.'** Explain why:

   The creature was relieved

   | 1 mark |

   ....

   The Morrisons were relieved

   | 1 mark |

   ....

3. Why do you think the TV repair man kept the creatures a secret?

   | 2 marks |

   ....

   ....

4. Do you think that the Gondrots get on well with inventors?
   Use evidence from the text to explain your answer. ← This means "write about the text in your answer".

   | 2 marks |

   ....

   ....

5. Write down **three** adjectives to describe the young Faraday. Explain each of your choices.

Adjective	**Explanation**
....	....
....	....
....	....

   | 3 marks |

Reading Raptors can answer Inference questions whilst hanging upside down. How did you get on?

A short extract from

The Gondrots

'We don't know a millionth of one percent about anything.'
Thomas Alva Edison

Prologue

Inside the TV, all was not well. A queasy feeling had overcome the operator and he was struggling to keep the television working properly. Before long his head began to spin and he dropped to the floor, exhausted. As he stopped working, so the TV stopped working. The Morrison family groaned as the picture flickered, fizzed and finally disappeared.

After Mr Morrison had bruised his toe kicking the wide-screen set, Mrs Morrison called the TV repair man. When he arrived, both the Morrisons and the creature inside the TV gave a sigh of relief.

'Ah yes, I see what your problem is,' said Ted the repair man. He gently lifted the small, dazed controller from inside the television. He was very careful to make sure that no one saw the creature being replaced.

The TV popped back into life and Ted began to screw the back on.

'Dust!' he lied. 'It gets everywhere and can wreak havoc with your internals if it builds up!' Ted knew he was lying. However, he didn't think he ought to tell the Morrisons that their television was operated from inside by a small creature.

He didn't think it would be wise to tell them that the creature was called a Gondrot.

He didn't think it would be suitable to tell them that Gondrots got their food through the wires and the plugs we insert into sockets.

He didn't think it would be a good idea to tell them that Gondrots and inventors had worked together for years.

He didn't think it would be clever to tell them that he was actually a government trained Gondrot doctor.

He didn't think they would believe him for a start!

The story continues over the page ➡

Chapter 1
Michael Faraday Meets the Gondrots

London 1812

The light from the candle hung in the air like a ghost, as the young man lit his way to the trap he had set. He heard dragging and scurrying sounds, then a powerful snap of metal as the mousetrap slammed down on its prey. He knew his invention had worked, but nothing could have prepared him for what he was about to see.

As he gazed down at his catch with its petal white skin and its leaf-like hair, the creature opened its wide brown eyes. Faraday screamed on a high note. He dropped his candle and ran for the door. The creature in the trap was frightened too but because his foot was caught, he couldn't run. Instead he picked himself up and hopped off into the dark cellar. The trap was firmly attached to his foot. He struggled through a hole in the skirting board, where his family was waiting for him.

'Did you get us some cheese, Wesley?' asked a similar looking creature with greener hair and a fatter belly.

'No, Snizzel!' snapped Wesley angrily. 'I dropped it when I got attacked by the contraption that's trying to swallow my foot as we speak! I do apologise!'

'OK, calm down,' replied Snizzel looking surprised. Snizzel was ruled by the sounds his belly made and right now it was making angry, grumbling ones.

The metal bar of the trap cracked down hard when Wesley pulled his foot free. Gondrots don't feel much pain. After he had given his leg a bit of a rub, Wesley began to think about his recent experience. What was the enormous creature that made such high-pitched noises? Was it strange for something so big to make sounds so small? He asked these questions because that was what he had been sent out to do — investigate and discover.

He took out his notebook and began making notes. He knew that there must be more of these large creatures. He made a mental note to hide whenever he saw one again, until he knew what they ate and how friendly they were. He didn't have long to wait though, before he saw one up close.

Michael Faraday knew that something unusual was living in his basement but he didn't know what. In his inventor's notebook he had written down some similar questions to Wesley. The next day found him creeping into the cellar to answer them. He was sure the creature had two arms, two legs and a head on top. He thought that its hair was made from leaves. Its skin seemed to be so white that it made him feel cold. But then again he hadn't really looked at it for long.

Faraday tip-toed into the basement and crept up to a hole in the skirting board, where he could hear noises. The small party of Gondrots were just waking up. They didn't hear the giant approach because they were so busy yawning, stretching, nibbling cheese and brushing their leafy hair.

As Faraday watched, he listened to the creatures. He heard himself described as 'a large squealing thing'. He disliked that. He had been taken by surprise and he couldn't help the noises he made! He also heard that the eldest member of their party, Latchett, had become very ill after eating some poisoned cheese. Faraday was alarmed because he had left the poisoned cheese down in the basement in the first place. He had thought it would get rid of the mice.

Faraday felt very guilty. He quietly got up and gathered his thoughts. He decided the best thing to do was to make some kind of contact with the creatures. He gathered together some cheese and fresh bread and placed it outside the skirting board. He knocked quite hard on the wall, hid behind a tall barrel and watched what happened next.

The deafening boom of Faraday's knocking stunned the Gondrots. It was a couple of minutes before they could hear each other speak again. Once his ears had resumed normal service, Wesley cautiously peered through the hole in the wall. He brushed his long green hair out of his eyes and checked to see if the world was still turning outside.

Faraday held his breath as the tiny head appeared through the hole. He was right! It did have leaves for hair. The brown eyes looked left, then right. Faraday thought they would pop when they saw the fresh food that he had left. As quick as a flash, Wesley was pushing the cheese back into the hole. He tried to do the same with the bread, but it was too big. He strained as he tried to push the bread into the hole. Faraday saw his chance to introduce himself.

Normally when two tribes meet for the first time, songs are sung and gifts are given. There are celebrations and flags are waved. But when human met Gondrot for the first time, things were very different. Faraday thought that the small creature would fall on his knees and gaze at the human's sheer size. He imagined that this moment would be memorable.

It was, but for all the wrong reasons!

'You'll never get it in if you don't cut it up,' said Faraday, not quite believing what he'd just said. Wesley let out a high-pitched scream and lurched forward. The lurch was so powerful that he ended up breaking the crust and landing inside the loaf itself. Trapped inside his doughy cage, Wesley screamed again. He was just about to eat his way out when he felt the loaf being lifted into the air. Suddenly the loaf was broken in two. Wesley found himself staring into the enormous eyes of the young Michael Faraday.

Wesley was embarrassed by his squeals. His leafy hair was full of bread crumbs. As he looked up at the giant inventor he wanted to say something fearsome and brave.

He wanted to, but he didn't. All he could manage was a medium-sized squeak that didn't make him sound very frightening at all.

So the great moment when human met Gondrot for the first time wasn't what it should have been. There was no singing and no flag waving. It certainly didn't suggest the fantastic relationship that was to come.

It was small and clumsy, a little bit like Wesley.

The Gondrots — Fiction

A piece of writing that's "fiction" <u>isn't</u> a true story. It's something written to entertain the people who read it. It could be a scary story, a funny story, even a confusing mystery. There's normally a bit of fiction in the SATs, so it's something to look forward to. A bit of the SATs that's actually fun. Wow...

What to do —

1) Open out the folding pages and read the story *The Gondrots*.

2) When you've read it, read it again.

3) After that, pretend you're a Gondrot for a few seconds, just to really get the feel of the story. Then stop messing about and get on with the questions.

Turn the page

 **AF6** # Writer's Purpose Questions

WRITER'S PURPOSE questions are about why the writer wrote what they did. We can't ask them, so we need to work it out ourselves. Read the story again and try these questions.

1. **'We don't know a millionth of one percent about anything.'**

Thomas Alva Edison was a very famous inventor. Why do you think the writer chose to include this quote and why did he put it in at the beginning of the story?

| 2 marks |

....

....

2. The author uses the prologue to

| introduce the main idea of the story | introduce us to the Morrison family | introduce us to the TV repair man | introduce us to the idea of Thomas Edison |

| 1 mark |

Circle your choice.

3. How would you describe this piece of writing? Tick a box and explain your answer underneath with reference to the text.

Funny ☐   Sad ☐   Serious ☐

| 3 marks |

....

....

....

....

4. The writer mentions that Faraday uses a candle, rather than an electric light. How does this help to set the scene for the reader?

| 1 mark |

....

Reading Raptors are always on the ball with Writer's Purpose questions. How did you do?

Language Questions

Writers choose their words and phrases carefully to make us feel a certain way. Read the story again and look out for any words that you find interesting. Then try these questions.

1. **'Faraday screamed on a high note.**
   He dropped his candle and ran for the door.'

   Underline three verbs in the sentences above that indicate
   Faraday's shock and actions.

   1 mark

2. How does the writer build up suspense in the first paragraph of Chapter 1?

   .... 2 marks

   ....

   ....

3. **'The light from the candle hung in the air like a ghost'**

   What does this phrase tell you about the atmosphere in the room?

   .... 2 marks

   ....

4. **'Its skin seemed to be so white that it made him feel cold.'**

   Explain why this description of the Gondrot's skin is effective.

   .... 1 mark

   ....

5. **'songs are sung and gifts given. There are celebrations and flags are waved'**

   Why does the writer describe what usually happens when two tribes meet?

   .... 2 marks

   ....

Language Questions

6. How does the phrase 'small and clumsy' describe the first meeting between Faraday and Wesley?

| 1 mark |

....

7. **'deafening boom'**

Why do you think the writer used this phrase and why do you think it is effective?

....

| 2 marks |

....

8. **'Faraday held his breath as the tiny head appeared through the hole. He was right! It did have leaves for hair.'**

| 1 mark |

Identify and underline the phrase the writer uses to create tension.

9. **'I dropped it when I got attacked by the contraption that's trying to swallow my foot as we speak! I do apologise!'**

Explain how the writer has used personification in this sentence.

....

| 2 marks |

....

10. **'The brown eyes looked left, then right.'**

Why does the writer use a short sentence here, and what effect does this have?

....

| 2 marks |

....

....

Reading Raptors find Language questions as easy as catching their dinner. How about you?

 **AF2**   # *Fact Retrieval Questions*

FACT RETRIEVAL is all about looking in the text and finding the answer. It's always there, somewhere... Have another read of the story and see if you can find the answers to these.

1. How did Mr Morrison bruise his toe?

| Tripping over the cat | Kicking the TV | Kicking the cat | Tripping over the TV |

`1 mark`

Put a ring around your answer.

2. What did the TV repair man say was the problem with the TV?

| Twisted wires | Blown fuse | Dust | Overheating |

`1 mark`

Put a ring around your answer.

3. What was really wrong with the television?

....

`1 mark`

4. a) How are the Gondrots in the TV fed?

....

`1 mark`

b) Ted is not really a TV repair man. What is his real job?

....

`1 mark`

5. Who was described as '**a large squealing thing**'?

| Mr Morrison | Michael Faraday | Wesley the Gondrot | Snizzel the Gondrot |

`1 mark`

Circle your answer.

Reading Raptors can retrieve facts quicker than they can say RAAAAAR! at a T-Rex. How did this page go?

The Wizard of Menlo Park

A Short Biography of The World's Greatest Inventor

Thomas Alva Edison

1847 – 1931

This is the story of Thomas Alva Edison, probably the world's greatest inventor. In his lifetime, he produced nearly 1400 patents. His inventions changed the way we see the world today and helped other inventors such as Marconi and Farnsworth to develop radio and television.

Edison spent every waking hour creating his own inventions and improving the inventions of others. He once famously said:

"Genius is one per cent inspiration and ninety nine per cent perspiration"

His words are a good description of his own life. When you read for yourself about the amazing life of this extraordinary inventor, I am sure you will understand why people believe that he was the greatest inventor the world has ever seen.

1847 – 1877

Thomas Alva Edison was born in Ohio, USA in 1847. He was an inquisitive child and he often asked questions that neither his mother nor his father could answer. By the age of ten, he had set up a chemical laboratory in the cellar of his home. By the age of twelve, he had got a part time job with the local railway company, selling newspapers to passengers on board the trains. He used the money he earned to buy more chemicals so he could continue his experiments.

Edison had a powerful imagination and a mind made for invention. By the time he was thirteen, he had set up his own newspaper called *The Weekly Herald* which he printed and published on the moving trains!

Turn the page ➡

Three years later, whilst still working for the railway company, he saved the life of a young boy who was almost crushed by a moving train. The boy turned out to be the son of the station telegrapher and, to return the favour, the boy's father taught Edison telegraphy.

Edison worked as a telegrapher until he was twenty one. His understanding of the machinery lead him to make his first invention – an electrical vote recorder. The machine made him his first real money and inspired him to continue on his great journey of invention.

At twenty four, working with another inventor called Sholes, Edison invented the first typewriter. Then in 1877, Edison produced one of his most famous inventions, and his own personal favourite, the phonograph.

EDISON FACTS

A telegrapher's job was to send short written messages called telegrams. Telegrams were sent using electrical currents with a code a bit like Morse code. They took only a few minutes to arrive, which was incredibly quick compared to a letter.

Telegraphers were very important people in Edison's time, because they could send these speedy messages anywhere in the world using the complicated electrical equipment.

EDISON FACTS

The phonograph was the very first record player. Edison used it to record the sound of his own voice on to a wax disc. The phonograph was wound up and a small needle was placed onto the wax disc. As the disc went round, he could hear his recording. The first thing Edison ever recorded was himself reciting the nursery rhyme 'Mary had a Little Lamb'.

  *The biography starts over the page*

1877 – 1905

Edison was becoming well known as an inventor. He moved to Menlo Park in New Jersey in 1879. He was at his most productive and successful there. At Menlo Park he invented the electric light bulb, electric sockets, electric switches and electric street lights.

He became known as 'the wizard of Menlo Park' after lighting up the streets outside his factory. His most unusual invention that year was gummed paper for sticking down envelopes!

Three years later he created an electric shaver, but that same year, 1891, brought another invention that started an industry. Thomas Edison invented the first motion picture camera and the movies were born.

Edison was a very hardworking man. He said that he never had enough time to do everything that he wanted to do — quite an amazing statement for a man who achieved so much.

By 1905 he had started work on X-ray machines and invented the first battery.

EDISON FACTS
The first films ever shown were silent movies. Edison's invention sparked the beginning of the silent film industry. It wasn't until later in his life that he developed a way of adding sound to film.

1906 – 1931

The final years of Edison's life found him improving on lots of early inventions. He spent time perfecting the phonograph and by 1912 had added sound to silent movies.

During World War 1, Edison was asked to contribute by helping the army develop underwater search lights and ways of detecting aeroplanes.

At the time of his death on October 18th 1931, Edison was still working. His many inventions had changed the way people lived. His favourite invention was the phonograph. "It speaks for itself," he said.

Many of the things we now take for granted would not be around if it wasn't for the incredible mind of Thomas Alva Edison.

← *Open the flap for the start of the biography*

SECTION 3 — THE WIZARD OF MENLO PARK — BIOGRAPHY

The Wizard of Menlo Park — Biography

Biographies are a type of non-fiction. A biography tells the story of someone's life. Very interesting things too, biographies. Some people have done some very exciting and amazing things. See if this biography inspires you to do some amazing things too, and maybe one day someone will write a biography about you.

What to do —

1) Open out the folding pages and read the biography *The Wizard of Menlo Park*.

2) When you've read it, sniff your socks — just to refresh yourself. Then read it again.

3) Then get on with the questions.

AF4

Structure and Layout Questions

STRUCTURE and LAYOUT questions are about how the story looks and what order things happen in. Flick through the story one more time before having a go at these questions.

1. The Prologue and Chapter 1 are made up of 5 main events. Number each stage to show the order in which they happen. The first one has been done for you.

	Faraday is frightened by his first sight of a Gondrot
	Faraday learns about Latchett and feels guilty
1	The Morrisons' television breaks down
	Faraday speaks to Wesley
	The repair man mends the TV

    2 marks

2. Why do you think the writer wrote the end of the Prologue in separate sentences?

    ....

    1 mark

AF7

Context Questions

CONTEXT questions are about how the text fits in with the world — where and when it's set and what sort of text it is. There's lots to think about, so you have to spot clues in the text.

1. Chapter 1 is set in 1812. Do you think the Prologue is set before or after this? Find **one** piece of evidence to support your answer.

    ....

    ....

    2 marks

2. Find **three** clues that tell you this is a fantasy story.

    a) ....

    b) ....

    3 marks

    c) ....

Reading Raptors know lots about the structure, layout and context of the things they read. How did you do?

AF2 *Fact Retrieval Questions*

If you've read the text really carefully, then FACT RETRIEVAL questions can be pretty simple — you just need to fish out the information that the questions ask for. Happy days.

1. What is this type of writing called?

| Fiction | Autobiography | Biography | Diary |

1 mark

Circle your answer.

2. In the first paragraph of the introduction, what does the writer describe Thomas Edison as?

....

1 mark

3. What was Thomas Edison's favourite invention?

| Phonograph | Telegraph | Light bulb | Street lights |

1 mark

Circle your answer.

4. In the section '**1877 - 1905**', what did Edison say that he didn't have enough of?

....

1 mark

5. At the end, the booklet tells us

| that Edison was soon forgotten after his death | that Edison's inventions have not been used since | that Edison invented things we still use today | that Edison didn't like any of his inventions |

1 mark

Circle your answer.

6. In what year did Edison move to Menlo Park?

....

1 mark

SECTION 3 — *THE WIZARD OF MENLO PARK* — BIOGRAPHY

© CGP 2012

AF2 **Fact Retrieval Questions**

7. Why did he become known as 'the wizard of Menlo Park'?

| He wore a pointed hat. | He lit up the streets outside his factory. | He chanted as he worked. | He told people to call him that. | 1 mark |

Circle your answer.

8. How many patents had Edison produced when he died?

1 mark

....

9. Use the information about Edison to match up the ages and dates with what happened then. The first one has been done for you.

By the time he was 10   Set up his own newspaper

1891   Built a chemical laboratory in his family cellar

By the time he was 13   Moved to Menlo Park

1879   Invented the motion picture camera

2 marks

10. Which of Edison's inventions started the film industry?

1 mark

....

11. Use the information about Edison to help you to fill in the spaces in this table.

	Tells us about the final years of Edison's life
Introduction	Builds up interest in the biography
1847 - 1877	
	Tells us about the busiest years of Edison's life

3 marks

Reading Raptors can find facts hidden in the middle of the biggest jungles. How did you get on?

SECTION 3 — THE WIZARD OF MENLO PARK — BIOGRAPHY

 # Structure and Layout Questions

STRUCTURE and LAYOUT questions are about how the text looks and how it's organised. Have another read of the text, paying attention to all that stuff, then try these.

1. Why do you think the writer put the **'Edison Facts'** in boxes and how do they help you to understand the text?

   ....

   ....

   2 marks

2. **'A Short Biography of The World's Greatest Inventor'**
   What is the purpose of this subheading?

   ....

   ....

   2 marks

3. There is no glossary in **'The Wizard of Menlo Park'**.
   Say whether you think the author should have included one and why.

   ....

   ....

   ....

   2 marks

4. How does the final sentence of the text link back to the introduction?
   What effect does this have?

   ....

   ....

   2 marks

5. Why do you think the writer breaks Edison's life up into sections?

   ....

   ....

   2 marks

Reading Raptors can do Layout questions whilst hopping on one leg. How did you do?

Writer's Purpose Questions

WRITER'S PURPOSE questions are all about working out why the author wrote what they did. Flick through the text and see if you can work out what the writer was thinking.

1. The introduction to this text

creates interest by describing Edison as the world's greatest inventor	tells us about other inventors who were like Edison	quotes some other inventors	sets the scene by describing where Edison lived

1 mark

Circle your answer.

2. 'Many of the things we now take for granted would not be around if it wasn't for the incredible mind of Thomas Alva Edison.'
What does this sentence tell you about the writer's opinion of Edison?

2 marks

....

....

3. 'He once famously said: "Genius is one per cent inspiration and ninety nine per cent perspiration". His words are a good description of his own life.'
Why do you think the writer says that this quote described Edison's life well?

3 marks

....

....

....

4. Why do you think the writer included quotations from Edison?

3 marks

....

....

....

Reading Raptors have a knack for working out exactly what writers are thinking. What about you?

AF3

Inference Questions

INFERENCE is different from fact retrieval — it's about understanding the things that the writer doesn't say directly. Read the text again and then have a go at these questions.

1. Which of the following ideas can be found in the text? Tick **two** boxes.

   ☐ **Edison worked really hard from an early age.**

   ☐ **Edison invented the television.**

   ☐ **Edison only used other people's ideas.**

   ☐ **Edison worked very long hours to achieve his success.**

   ☐ **Edison created the first computer.**

   `2 marks`

2. The writer says that Edison became known as **'the wizard of Menlo Park'**. What does this suggest about people's feelings towards Edison's inventions?

   ....

   ....

   `2 marks`

3. **'His favourite invention was the phonograph. "It speaks for itself," he said.'** What do you think Edison meant by this phrase?

   ....

   ....

   `2 marks`

4. The writer describes Edison as an **'extraordinary inventor'**. Using evidence from the text, show why the writer thinks that Edison is extraordinary.

   ....

   ....

   ....

   `2 marks`

Reading Raptors can do Inference questions while standing on stilts and juggling. How did you get on?

The last few questions on *The Wizard of Menlo Park* are under here ➤

Turn the page

Winds of Change — Newspaper Article

Newspaper articles are a slippery mixture of facts, opinions and arguments.
Read the article, and read it all over again. Then you can try the questions.

Not all inventions are welcomed with enthusiasm — sometimes it takes people time to work out how new inventions will help them. Once they get used to them, they often forget what all the fuss was about. The newspaper article below shows how an exciting invention can upset small communities.

Winds of Change

Villagers angry about damage to 'beauty spot'

Tempers are running high in the normally sleepy Somerset village of Little Crampton. The local electricity company, Weslec, have decided to install a wind farm of over thirty wind turbines on hillsides overlooking the village.

Wind farm will produce pollution-free electricity

The wind farm will create pollution-free electricity for the community. Since its invention in 1888 by Charles Brush, the wind turbine has been a widely-used form of technology. Wind farms have been used for many years by communities in both Europe and America. Since sleeker and quieter models were created by the French inventor Darrieus, they have been seen more frequently in the UK.

Villager Mat Elland, however, is unimpressed by the wind turbines' importance as a major invention. He told us:

'Those wind thingies are an eyesore. They're going to ruin our views and frighten our animals. It shouldn't be allowed.'

Clashes at public meeting

At a meeting of villagers in the local pub, many opinions were heard. Most of those present were against the development. Even when Weslec president Andrew Bell made the case for the wind farm, few were convinced. Mr Bell's speech was short but clear:

'We cannot continue creating pollution. Our wind farm will make pollution-free electricity for the people of Little Crampton and beyond. That means that your children will be breathing cleaner air and your electricity will be environmentally friendly. That is something you can be proud of.'

After the meeting, Mr Bell told us: 'I can understand why people are upset, but the benefits are far greater than the losses. People have got to wake up to the reality of alternative energy. Inventors have offered us fantastic solutions to the problem of pollution and we should embrace them.'

Local council welcomes the development

The plans to develop the wind farm are yet to be fully decided but the local council welcomes the development.

Councillor Jake Roberts told us:

'These types of thing quickly become tourist attractions and that brings money into the villages.'

The final say, however, will come from the Government.

A public meeting was held at this pub

Local priest Harry Weightman spoke about the feeling in the community:

'I think we are angry because we don't feel our opinions are valued. I've lived in this village for fifty years and the beautiful countryside that surrounds me could soon be changed forever. It's a very worrying time for me.'

Whatever happens at Little Crampton, the villagers have shown how much they value their local countryside. It appears, however, that the need to conserve areas of beauty by protecting them from pollution has not yet been fully understood. When it is, hopefully opinions about the wind farm will change.

AF5

Language Questions

LANGUAGE questions are all about how the writer uses words to make us feel a certain way.
Writers are very sneaky like that. Have a final read of the text and try these questions.

1. **'When you read for yourself about the amazing life of this extraordinary inventor, I am sure you will understand why people believe that he was the greatest inventor the world has ever seen.'**

   Underline the adjectives that create the impression that Edison was a special man.

   `1 mark`

2. a) Tick a box below to show whose point of view the introduction on page 23 is written from.

   The author ☐   Thomas Edison ☐

   `1 mark`

   b) What effect do you think this has?

   ....

   `1 mark`

   ....

3. **'By the time he was thirteen, he had set up his own newspaper called *The Weekly Herald* which he printed and published on the moving trains!'**

   Why do you think the writer uses an exclamation mark at the end of this paragraph and what does this tell you about how he feels about the inventor?

   ....

   `2 marks`

   ....

4. **'Edison spent every waking hour creating his own inventions and improving the inventions of others.'**

   Why do you think the writer chose the phrase **'every waking hour'** to describe Edison's life?

   ....

   `2 marks`

   ....

Reading Raptors find Language questions more
fun than playing hopscotch. How did you get on?

AF3 | ## Inference Questions

INFERENCE questions ask you to work things out using a bit of imagination. Read through the text again and see if you can work out the answers to these questions.

1. The villagers think Weslec are

acting considerately and thinking of the environment	acting generously and giving people money	not listening to what people have to say	listening carefully to concerns and acting on them

1 mark

Put a ring around your choice.

2. Why do you think Harry Weightman has strong opinions about the wind farm?

....

1 mark

3. Why do you think Councillor Jake Roberts is happy that money will be coming into the village?

....

1 mark

4. Mat Elland feels

angry	hopeful	frightened	uncertain

Put a ring around your choice and explain your answer below.

2 marks

....

....

5. Do you think Harry Weightman is more concerned for himself than the village? Explain your answer fully.

2 marks

....

....

Reading Raptors can always work out what the writer's on about. How did you get on with these questions?

AF5   *Language Questions*

These LANGUAGE questions are about why the author uses certain words and phrases and what they are trying to make you think or feel. Have a go at answering them.

1. Why do you think the writer describes Little Crampton as **'sleepy'**?

....

1
mark

2. **'Clashes at public meeting'**

Do you think this heading is effective? Explain your answer.

....

2
marks

....

3. **'Those wind thingies are an eyesore.'**

    a) What impression does the word **'thingies'** give?

....

2
marks

....

    b) Why is the word **'eyesore'** effective?

1
mark

....

4. What does the title **'Winds of Change'** mean? Do you think it is a good title? Explain your answer as fully as you can.

....

....

3
marks

....

....

Reading Raptors can do Language questions as soon as they've hatched out of the egg. How did you do?

     SECTION 4 — WINDS OF CHANGE — NEWSPAPER ARTICLE

Fact Retrieval Questions

FACT RETRIEVAL questions are about picking out the right bits of information from all the stuff the text is telling you. See if you can pick out the answers to these questions.

1. Why is Mat Elland against the wind farm?

    ....

    1 mark

2. Why is Andrew Bell in favour of the wind farm?

    ....

    1 mark

3. Write down three main points that are made in favour of the wind farm.

    ....

    ....

    ....

    3 marks

4. The wind turbine was invented by Charles Brush in

1777	1999	2000	1888

    1 mark

    Put a ring around your choice.

5. Why is Councillor Jake Roberts in favour of the wind farm?

    ....

    1 mark

6. How many wind turbines have Weslec decided to install near Little Crampton?

Over ten	Over twenty	Over thirty	Over forty

    1 mark

    Put a ring around your choice.

Reading Raptors can find facts hidden deep inside piranha-infested swamps. How did you get on?

© CGP 2012

Writer's Purpose Questions

Writers often have an opinion on a topic and this affects what they write about it. Have another read of the article and think about the writer's view on wind turbines.

1. What is the main purpose of this text?

to show how inventions can upset communities	to show how large wind turbines are	to show how dangerous wind turbines are	to show that people in villages always argue

1 mark

Circle your answer.

2. Why do you think the writer included the opinions of four different people?

1 mark

....

3. Why did the writer include the history of the wind turbine in the article?

2 marks

....

....

4. 'When it is, hopefully opinions about the wind farm will change.'

What does this sentence tell you about the writer's opinion?

1 mark

....

5. Do you think this is a biased newspaper report?

Refer to the text in your answer.

....

3 marks

....

....

Reading Raptors can always work out why authors have written certain things. How did you do?

SECTION 4 — WINDS OF CHANGE — NEWSPAPER ARTICLE

AF2 # Questions On The Whole Lot

Now it's time to think about all the texts together. You might have to compare one text with another, so give them all another read before you try to answer these questions.

1. In which text would you find information about Thomas Alva Edison?

The Wizard of Menlo Park	Winds of Change	The Gondrots	Eureka!

Circle your answer.

2. Where would you find information about Sir Isaac Newton?

The Wizard of Menlo Park	Winds of Change	The Gondrots	Eureka!

Circle your answer.

3. Where would you find information about wind turbines?

The Wizard of Menlo Park	Winds of Change	The Gondrots	Eureka!

Circle your answer.

4. Match up each sentence to the type of writing it came from.

The plans to develop the wind farm are yet to be fully decided but the local council welcomes the development.

Fiction

As he gazed down at his catch with its petal white skin and its leaf-like hair, the creature opened its wide brown eyes.

Biography

He used the money he earned to buy more chemicals so he could continue his experiments.

Newspaper article

E6R122